Written By: Charron Monaye © 2019

Published By: Pen Legacy®

Cover & Formatting By: The Liar's Craft

Edited By: U Can Mark My Word Editorial Services

ALL RIGHTS RESERVED. No part of this book may be reproduced in any written, electronic, recording, or photocopying without written permission of the publisher or author. The exception would be in the case of brief quotations embodied in the critical articles or reviews and pages where permission is specifically granted by the publisher or author.

DISCLAIMER

Although you may find the teachings, life lessons and examples in this book to be useful, the book is sold with the understanding that neither the author nor Pen Legacy® are engaged in presenting any legal, relationship, financial, emotional, or health advice.

Any person who's experiencing financial, anxiety, depression, health, or relationship issues should consult with a licensed therapist, advisor, licensed psychologist, or any qualified professional before commencing into anything described in this book. This book's intent is to provide you with the writer's account and experience with overcoming life matters. All results will differ than yours; however, our goal is to provide you with our "take" on how to overcome and be resilient when faced with circumstances. There are lessons in every blessing.

Library of Congress Cataloging – in- Publication Data has been applied for.

ISBN:

PRINTED IN THE UNITED STATES OF AMERICA.

Also by Charron Monaye

BOOKS

2018 Legacy Journal & Planner: A Planning Tool for your Freedom & Future

I Matter Journal

STOP Asking for Permission & Give Notice: How to Accept & Attain Who You Are Without Validation

Love the Real You: Uncovering Your "WHY" & Affirming You're Enough

UnBreak My Heart: From Scorn to Finding Love Again

My Side of the Story: From a Woman Waiting to Exhale

Bruised, Broken, and Blessed, compiled by Charron Monaye & Shontaye Hawkins

Get Out of Your Own Way, compiled by Charron Monaye

Secure Your Legacy Journal

STAGE PLAYS

Get Out of Your Own Way

Why Can't We Be Friends

Living Your Life

CO-AUTHORED BOOK

The Woodshed, by Jaguar Wright

Books are available on Amazon, Barnes & Noble, Books-A-Million, Wal-Mart

F.E.A.R

Is A Crime

CHARRON MONAYE

PEN LEGACY DECLARATION OF PERSONAL FREEDOM

I, _____, from this day forward confess my commitment to myself, my dreams, and my goals, and I vow to stay the course to my personal freedom and legacy. Fear no longer has a place in my life. I will not allow anyone, including myself, to keep me from living the life I want. I AM committed to doing the work on myself so that I can enjoy life, live to my fullest potential, and be remembered for my offerings, love, and greatest qualities. I pledge to:

1. Be honest with myself throughout this process.
2. Gain clarity of who I am so I can be clear on what I want and how to receive it.
3. Engage with only positive, life-minded individuals who will provide support during my journey.
4. Attend at least one empowerment and financial workshop.
5. Obtain a life coach or accountability partner to help me stay on course.
6. Save 10% and invest 15% of my income.
7. Commit to traveling to a city/state that I've never been once every quarter.
8. Face Everything And Rise.

I AM committed to this unwavering and personal covenant.

SIGNATURE:
_____

DATE:
_____

F.E.A.R CONTENTS

What Are Your Rights?

2

Opening Statement

3

Who is Charron & Why Should You Read This Book?

5

What is F.E.A.R.?

11

How to Change a Projected Mindset

22

How to Break the Chains

44

Face Everything And Rise

74

Set the Intention

96

Verdict

101

Mission Accomplished

111

About the Author

128

WHAT ARE YOUR RIGHTS?

"You have the right to remain silent. Anything you say can and will be used against you in a court of law. You have the right to an attorney. If you cannot afford an attorney, one will be provided for you. You have the ability to reject fear. For anything you are about to go through will work out for your good. Do you understand the rights I have just read to you? With these rights in mind, do you wish to speak to me?"

OPENING STATEMENT

Good day, ladies and gentlemen. My name is Charron Monaye, and I am representing the plaintiff, YOU. We are here today to decide if the defendant, FEAR, is liable for damages caused to your life as a result of procrastination, self-sabotaging thoughts, denial, overspending, complacency and delay.

On that day when you were given the opportunity to do better, achieve more, and live the life you desire, you declined. We will provide factual evidence, coaching questions, and mindset-shift challenges that will show you how—and where—you gave FEAR permission to step in and take over. Also, we will provide the compelling eyewitness testimony of FAITH, who saw the defendant's motive. Ladies and gentlemen of the jury, FEAR is a hardworking, honest, and law-abiding citizen that often sucks the life out of people, but is invited in and allowed to terminate life.

At the conclusion of this book, I hope that in the interest of justice, you will find that the defendant is responsible for causing YOUR setbacks and therefore will find favor with choosing and trusting yourself.

WHO IS CHARRON & WHY SHOULD YOU READ THIS BOOK?

At the beginning of my coaching sessions, I shock people when one of the first things I tell them is, "Don't believe a word I say." Why would I suggest that? Because I can only speak from my personal experiences. None of the concepts and insights I share are inherently true or false, right or wrong. They merely reflect my results and the amazing results I've seen in the lives of my clients. However, I believe if you do the work and apply the concepts you learn in this book, you will transform your life. Don't just read this book. Study it as if your life depends on it. Then, try the principles out for yourself. Whatever works, keep doing. Whatever doesn't, you're welcome to throw away.

I know I may be biased, but when it comes to fear, this may be the most important book you'll ever read. Sure, that might be a bold statement, but the fact is, this book provides the missing link between your desire for success and your achievement of success. As you've probably found out by now, those are two different worlds. No doubt you've read other books, listened to CDs or podcasts, taken courses, and learned about how to "Live Your Best Life". But, what happened? For most people, not much! They get a short blast of energy, and then it's back to the status quo. Finally, there's an answer. It's simple, it's law, and you're not going to circumvent it. It all comes down to this: if your subconscious "fearless blueprint" is not "set" for success, nothing you learn, nothing you know, and nothing you do will make much of a difference.

In the pages of this book, we will demystify why some people are destined to be courageous while others are destined for a life of struggle. You will gain awareness of the root causes of fear, an unmotivated mindset, or stagnation so you can begin changing your future for the better. You will understand how childhood influences shape our sense of fear and how these influences have led to self-defeating thoughts and habits. You will experience powerful declarations that will help you replace your limited ways of thinking with mental "wealth files" so that you think—and succeed—as fearless people do. You will also learn practical, step-by-step strategies for increasing your motivation and building a greater sense of purpose. But, the unique thing about this book is, I will be presenting this lesson in the form of a court case. US vs. FEAR! You got it! Fear is on trial, and we finally get to present our case, understand fear's argument, listen to witnesses' testimonies, and finally get to determine fear's fate in our lives.

Now I know you must be thinking, so what is your experience? Where are you coming from? Were you always successful?

I wish! Like many of you, I supposedly had a lot of "potential" but had little to show for it. I read numerous books, listened to many tapes, and went to countless women empowerment conferences. I really, really, really wanted to live the life I had envisioned for myself. I don't know whether it was for the money, the freedom, the sense of achievement, or to prove I was good enough in my parents' eyes, but I was almost obsessed with becoming a "success". During my thirties, I started my writing journey. I began as a songwriter, then progressed to authoring books, later tapping into being a playwright and finally a blogger. I worked my butt off but kept coming up short. I kept thinking, *If I'm such a great writer, why aren't my books and play making me millions?* No matter what industry I tried to jump in, nothing was working as fast as I needed it to be…at least not for me. It was the last part of that sentence that finally struck me. How come others were succeeding in the same business I was in, yet I was still broke, hustling?

So, I began doing some serious soul-searching. I examined my true beliefs and saw that even though I wanted to be a writer, I had some deep-rooted apprehensions about it. Mostly, I was afraid I might fail. I had already invested so much into this writing goal that if I failed, everyone who doubted me would have given me the "I told you so" speech. Then, I got some advice from my pastor Rev. Dr. Jerome F. Coleman's sermons when I attended church and by listening to Sara Jake Roberts. They all said the same thing: "God is not going to bless you with what you desire until you prove you appreciate what you have." This advice changed my life. What I wanted was not in reach because I had never taken the time to see, love, and be grateful for the opportunities I had and am still receiving.

As I thought about it all, the fear of losing was mute. My biggest issue was I did not believe in myself enough to know I was worthy. Finally, in 2017, I said, "Enough yakking about it. Let's put it to the test." That's when I decided to produce my play "Get Out of Your Own Way," which debuted in Hollywood, California, from Abington, Pennsylvania. I connected with an actress, who starred in my first play and had relocated to California, to see if she would direct it. Low and behold, she agreed, and that was the start of my fearless life. I pushed fear and lack of believing to the side, and I dived in with no money, a small budget, and a lot of faith. The play premiered October 5, 2018, and ran until October 7th. With three sold-out shows, tons of positive feedback, and love from the audience, I boarded my return flight feeling like a new woman although I was now forty years of age. Can you believe it? It took me ten years to fully believe in myself and start living a fulfilled life, not just a content one. Are you ready to fully believe in yourself?

Even though I suggest that you don't believe a word I say and to instead test these concepts out for yourself, I'm going to ask you to trust the ideas you will read in this. Not because you know me personally, but because thousands of people have already changed their lives as a result of the principles in this book. Speaking of trust, it reminds me of one of my favorite stories about a man who is walking along a cliff and suddenly loses his balance, slips, and falls off. Fortunately, he has the presence of mind to grab on to the ledge, and he's hanging there for dear life. He continues to hang until he finally yells, "Is there anybody up there who can help me?" There's no answer. He keeps calling out, "Is there anybody up there who can help me?" Finally, a bellowing voice calls back, "This is God. I can help you. Just let go and trust." Next thing you hear is the man yelling, "Is there anybody *else* up there who can help me?" The lesson is simple. If you want to move to a higher level of life, you have to be willing to let go of some of your old ways and adopt new ones. The results will eventually speak for themselves.

WHAT IS F.E.A.R.?

FEAR! This word has become the #1 reason why individuals deny themselves the right to their unalienable rights of Life, Liberty, and the Pursuit of Happiness. Before I continue my stand on this, let's define the word so we can be clear on the charges presented. According to Dictionary.com, fear is defined as "a distressing emotion aroused by impending danger, evil, pain, etc., whether the threat is real or imagined; the feeling or condition of being afraid; something that causes feelings of dread or apprehension; something a person is afraid of." But, on the flip side, "fear is an element that is needed to keep you cautious in life." Ah ha! So, fear can appear in the form of apprehension, projected or cautionary. But, for some reason, you have managed to use it as a form of apprehension only, which is why you are spinning in circles rather than enjoying the life given to you. Let's examine the two so that you can start gaining clarity on your path to freedom.

Apprehension

If you're anything like me, you can become extremely doubtful to the point of allowing worry to deny you access to what you want. I can remember when I started as an entrepreneur. I had many big dreams, such as making the New York Times Best Seller list and receiving a Tony Award for one of my plays. I wanted to relocate from Philadelphia and start anew somewhere in the world, where people respected my talent and loved me for who I am as a person. I wanted so much for myself. However, instead of going after those things that I desired, I allowed the fear projected on me—by myself and others—to stop me dead in my tracks. Instead of living, I existed as a federal employee because my parents drilled in me that job security, pension, and having a job was more important than living out your uncertain dreams. I played small to keep my pen writing, and I existed just enough to stay happy. But, how do you think that made me feel mentally and emotionally? To have a bag of dreams that you give up on is heartbreaking, but walking in fear of "what ifs" is life-ending. By remaining in my comfortable state, I never gave myself permission to try my luck–to seriously bet on me and my goals of becoming a prominent writer.

On top of that, I am a mother of two children and the primary custodian of both. So, in addition to having a job, I had children who depended on me. Sure, their father supported them, but I was their present parent, their mother—and any time away from them played on my guilt. I used to hear stuff like, "We're from the old school. Mothers stop living their lives when they have a child." Right after college, at the age of twenty-three, I became a mother. So, I had to stop living just for myself. Or so I thought! Then at twenty-nine years of age, I gave birth to my baby boy. That's when I thought, *That's it! Charron who? Charron what?* I no longer mattered, but that wasn't necessarily true. Being a single mother and trying to provide for children who have big appetites for life, I had to figure out a way to provide for them without having to say "no" to a majority of their request.

Despite having a job, I was still broke. What was I going to do? It came to a point where I had to make a decision. I could stay and struggle knowing the end game, or while remaining employed, I could bet on my gift to see if it could make room for me. In 2008, while praying and crying to God for deliverance from an eviction, shut-off utilities, and an empty refrigerator, my oldest son Chris handed me a composition book that I used to write in and said, "Mommy, write about it." HIS WORDS SHOCKED ME! How could this six-year-old boy have more faith in me than I had in myself? Did he know what would come with this writing? The time away from home! The financial investment that may return nothing! Did he know what he was offering? Hell, was I up for the challenge of trying to build my dream as a writer? Remember, I work for the government. So, with having a nine-to-five, when would I find time to write, travel, and network? I finally decided if fear got me there, then my son's faith could save us.

For years, fear stopped me from living. It prevented me from trusting my first love when he chose to join the army. Instead of trusting him and his new life, I stayed back and called off our engagement because of what others thought about his decisions and actions. *He ran off to join the military and left you? He was cheating with her; that's why he married her so fast. Her first baby is his.* Can you tell that I lived my life solely on the principle of "what if" and what others said, but then cried when I lost out and was forced to watch while others enjoyed what was supposed to be mine? However, while writing my book titled *Stop Asking for Permission & Give Notice*, I realized in my moment of clarity that fear caused my apprehension and kept me asking for permission. Not permission from myself but others, mainly my family. I did not believe or have enough faith in myself to trust that what was presented to me was presented for a reason. There is never any harm in trying and learning, but I denied myself that effort to embrace what society and tradition deemed normal.

Now, what do you think would've happened if I moved on my dreams but proceeded with caution? Moving in faith, but with options, preparedness, and plans. Would that be wrong? Would I be a bad mother? What would people say about me? And although I still didn't have my love, if God granted us another chance, I would be all over it. How did I get to this place of fear? Before we learn more to answer this question properly, let's get clear on what we lost because of apprehensive fear.

Coaching Moment!

Where would you be right now, at this moment, if you did not give fear permission to live your life? Without projected fear or your self-inflicted fear, where would you be? What did you say "no" to that should've been a "yes"? What did you let go of instead of trusting that everything would work out?

_____
_____
_____
_____
_____

Projected

This form of fear, in my opinion, is the #1 dream killer of people, no matter their age, especially those who seek validation from others. For example, have you ever been to a playground and watched how fearless children are? They play in the mud, pick up bugs with their bare hands, hang upside down from the monkey bars, and swing dangerously. They even engage in rough play sometimes. They get hurt and cry for a minute, but then they go right back to doing the same thing that got them hurt before. They fear nothing! But, have you ever witnessed a mother or father at the playground telling their child not to swing on the monkey bars because they "look" dangerous. It's not that they *are* dangerous, but because they *look* dangerous, they project their fear of their child getting hurt on them, which stops the child from playing on it. Have you witnessed this? Have you done it? I remember when my son used to go over my ex-husband's mother's house. She used to let him pick bugs. Chris would have a ball, but the mother in me—and hater of insects—caused me to object and always make him find something else to do. Who knows, his love of bugs could have led to him becoming an entomologist, but I denied him that.

For many of us, we are living with projected fear, which is one of the hardest fears to break since it is taught. Everything you were taught that has you now second-guessing your desires and dreams are projected. Just like I mentioned previously, the importance of job security and motherhood was projected on me, which left me to embrace surviving in an unhappy state! I almost felt like having children was a curse because everything that once brought me joy was out of reach. Then I was told how my government job was golden and that I better not leave this place no matter how much it stresses me! *Stress is nothing compared to receiving a great paycheck every other Friday*, they would say. Was my government job all that I was living for, though? Projected! Every day when I came home from work, I would cry because I knew there was more to life. But, how do you change your mindset into believing you are worthy of more when the guidelines for being an adult and mother have been embedded in you? If your upbringing was anything like mine, you were told that once you turned eighteen, your goals at that point were to:

- **Get married (optional)**
- **Go to college**
- **Get a job**

- **Retire**

When do you achieve your dreams, fulfill goals, travel the world, or walk into your talents? Are you living only to get up, eat, go to work, come home, eat, and go to bed, and if you are a person of faith, attend church on Sunday? This kind of projection has kept many individuals, like me, stuck and hoping for better, not realizing that the better we seek is within us and involves us getting up and doing something other than what's been projected on us. But, how do you change your mindset? I had to ask myself that question, too. But, I praise God that I was able to get the answers, apply them to myself, and am now living with no fear. I even had to reprogram my children's way of thinking so they would have the opportunity to live and learn, instead of feeling like a failure "if" things don't go their way. Through experience, I adopted five mind-changing declarations that keep me in my life of movement, even when projected fear is presented.

- **I Believe in Myself**
- **I See Failure as Learning Blocks, Not The End**
- **What God Has for Me, It Is for Me**
- **I Can Only Achieve What I Try To Do**
- **There's a Whole World Out Here; Never Stay Within Your Four Walls for Long**

Cautionary

Now, this form of fear should be used to be careful when making decisions during your pursuit of things. Taking caution is another way of staying alert and prepared. This is how I choose to use fear in my life today. When my son handed me the composition book and told me to write, I had a decision to make. Maintain my apprehension? (Remember the projected fears!) Or trust my son enough to proceed cautiously. Choosing to be cautious led me to create the "fearless formula" that I still live by today.

Plan + Pray + Prepare = Execute

From that moment forward, I agreed to learn, experiment, and invest what I had to offer to start the train moving. In 2009, I started writing song lyrics. 2010, my first book was published. 2012, I wrote and co-produced my very first play. 2015, I created Pen Legacy Publishing, and in 2018, I wrote, produced, and premiered my play in Hollywood, California. In between these milestones, I was awarded Best Independent Author, authored ten books, co-authored four, published over twenty-five new authors, written/produced three theatrical productions, contributed to more than twenty book anthologies, and hired to pen other theatrical scripts. Additionally, I was formerly a staff writer for the Philadelphia

Association of Paralegals & CNN iReport, featured contributor on GovLoop.com, and Editor-In-Chief for www.madisonjaye.com. I proved to myself that I could work have a career, be a mother, and in 2015, maintain a relationship with my former love while still achieving my dreams. Remind you, I have been writing since the age of fourteen, but it took me seventeen years to step outside of the ritual of fear and self-doubt to be who I was destined to be finally. With the demands of my career, I sometimes had to leave my children and would miss some of their events. However, I am blessed to have children who not only look for me to encourage and push them, but they also motivate me.

So, knowing the three forms of fear—apprehension, projected, and cautionary—with which one do you struggle? Fear is not supposed to be a hindrance in your life. Instead, use it as a tool to protect yourself. Today, I look at fear as God's protection. I pray on everything I want before I pursue it, and if my plan does not come back as a valid one, then I try to address the issues and readjust. Sometimes moving in caution makes you readjust, and in that, I have found that you usually create the better version of what you initially thought was good.

When you live in full knowing,
you allow the true spirit of fear to keep you cautious in life.
When you're careful, you soar.

HOW TO CHANGE A PROJECTED MINDSET?

Let's go back down memory lane for a minute. When did you get introduced to fear, and how old were you? How did that experience change your life? When we think of fear, we tend to think we've always been afraid of stuff, but the truth is, fear is an element of life and something that grows as you evolve as a person. Think about it; babies and toddlers are not afraid of much of anything. They will get hurt and go back to the very thing that hurt them. They will jump off of high structures and play with sharp objects. They terrorize pets. They live and enjoy life, not necessarily paying attention to the consequences of their actions or the danger around them. They live with no regrets, then go to sleep when they've had enough.

So why do you think we lost that concept of living? Is it because we learn that consequences hurt or that every action comes with a price? But, who's to say that fear's price is always costly? Or it is it because our parents, friends, teachers, or—depending on the era you came up in—the whole neighborhood that acted as your guardian, projected their fears of what could happen on you. Now, don't get me wrong. I'm not saying we should allow children to do things that will ultimately cause them harm, but we should not try to protect them so much that we stop them from living either. For example, my mother, as a teenager, had a horrific incident involving swimming that almost caused her to drown. Welp, there went me and my sister's chances of learning how to swim or going down by the ocean when we went to the beach. The boardwalk life is amazing, right? Wrong! That projected fear made us respect her fear of large bodies of water and not indulge. To this day, I don't know how to swim, even though both my children do. As parents, you would be surprised just how much we project to our children. From your habits to your attitude, to the way you handle people, your children will adapt to your demeanor because it's what they see and hear.

For example, I can remember being a person who would conform instead of arguing. I am not a confrontational person, and whenever I dealt with someone who was, I would give in and accept whatever to regain peace again. Unbeknownst to me, Chris had picked up that same behavior, and I almost died knowing I was the cause. Seeing Chris cry because he felt compelled to do something that he did not want to do made me livid. Knowing this feeling all too well, I set my focus on learning how to break this trait.

After seeing my son living in the shadow of my bad traits, I began studying the idea of "projecting" and learned that this concept fell under the term psychological projection. Psychological projection involves projecting undesirable feelings or emotions onto someone else rather than admitting to or dealing with unwanted feelings. Sigmund Freud, an Austrian psychologist, developed the theory of psychological projection. During his sessions with patients, Freud noticed that they would sometimes accuse others of having the same feelings they themselves were demonstrating. A classic example of Freudian projection is that of a woman who has been unfaithful to her husband but who accuses him of cheating on her. How many of you are guilty of this one? I know I am. But, we often put it off as having trust issues. No, when you have unresolved issues within you, you feel that everything and everyone is guilty. According to everydayhealth.com, "psychological projection is one of many defense mechanisms people engage in on a regular basis." So, we project as a mean to defend our wrongs, thus giving us the opportunity to live with negativity, fear, anger, and other emotions that can keep us and others just existing. Plus, projection permits us to stay the victim. Therefore, instead of addressing the situation, we create more victims of circumstances because they are only projecting what they learned and not what they know to be true. Think about it, how many lives have you hindered because of what was projected on you and what you now defend? Are you preaching for someone to work a 9-to-5 job because you honestly think it's the best way to earn a living or because it's what you were told?

Coaching Moment!

What were some of the things told to you by your parents or family members that you continue to live by in your adult life?

_____
_____
_____
_____
_____
_____
_____
_____

What are some of the things you are projecting now as an adult that you feel should be your child(ren)'s decision to make?

_____
_____
_____
_____
_____
_____
_____
_____

What do you need to change? Are you the reason why your child is struggling, or are you stuck praying for your breakthrough? Can I share a secret with you? The ticket to your breakthrough is removing all of the stuff that you "think" will happen if you move outside of comfortability. Transitioning from what you know to the unknown is already a scary event, but not for a child or person who is committed to having fun. Are you ready to experience unapologetic fun, fearless living, and unshakable faith? Can you live not knowing where your next meal is going to come from, but knowing that God is able? Are you willing to erase what you thought you knew to be true?

When I turned that composition book into a published book, I didn't know what was going to come from it, but I knew the projected life I was living wasn't taking me anywhere fast. Matter fact, I was no different than the people who projected their concepts on me. We were all broke—robbing Peter to pay Paul, gossiping, praying for better, and complaining about our jobs. Is it me, or does it seem like everyone who projected their fears onto you isn't doing that much better than you? I mean, it's like they try to diminish your life so they can have company in theirs. Have you noticed that? Or is this new to you? Take a minute and think about everyone who has projected onto you. Where are they at now in their life? Interesting, right?

So how do we stop projecting and allowing projecting in our lives? We have touched on how fear starts, but how do we stop it? The answers are simple:
- Don't be afraid to step outside of the "traditional" comfort zone. It's a better view from the side of freedom.
- Understand that everyone has a life. Live yours so that you don't have to live vicariously through them.
- Be aware that people project their failures onto you to prevent you from "achieving" what will never happen.
- Everyone has an opinion of what will work in life; only trust what you know to be true.

- Use what you need from the lessons you learned to propel you forward, and trust your instincts.

I can go on and on, but to propel past projection, you must believe in you. Trust in yourself enough to know that you hold the key to your desires and most importantly your destiny. Also, examine the negative relationships in your life. Negativity is projected, and therefore, you must eradicate it from your life. Family, friends, co-workers, or social media friends—anyone who is negative must go. The less negativity you hear and the more you exercise having a winning attitude, the less you will fear and the more success you will experience.

WHAT IS FAITH?

Even though there is a worldly definition of faith, in my opinion, Hebrew 11:1 is by far the best description of what faith is. Hebrew 11:1 says, "Now faith is confidence in what we hope for and assurance about what we do not see." Before we move forward, what are some things you hoped for but let slip away because of your fear? How many times has your faith been tested because what you hoped for and the reality of a situation didn't add up? Things you once believed were possible are now being deemed as impossible, thus giving you the spirit of quit. Are you in the spirit of quit right now? Or are you still working towards that goal, that promotion, or something else that will bring greater to your life?

Because you have to believe what you don't see, I know firsthand just how hard it is to move on faith. I can remember taking a millionaire mastery class with multi-millionaire David Imonitie Jr., who spoke on the importance of faith from the spiritual aspect. He stressed that "your faith is the only way to communicate and get a response out of God." When you are looking for things to change, you have to possess mustard seed faith, knowing that what you want and need is coming. Some of us lose faith because of our lack of patience. However, if we realized our patience allows us to prepare and work, we would save ourselves a lot of stress and grief. As I fought with keeping my faith and having more faith in the unseen, I learned to capitalize and leverage the work I had to do in the meantime. Manifesting, Patience, Environment, and Work are the ingredients of sustaining between Asking and Receiving. It's almost like an equation:

Ask (Faith) → **Manifesting, Patience, Environment, Work** → **Receive** (I have it!)

Faith is like planting a seed and waiting for it to grow. You have no idea where and how it will start sprouting; you just know it will. You need to have that kind of faith in your life. That's the faith that wins the game. Before we move forward, let's explore what you should be doing in the meantime during our period of waiting.

Manifesting

Manifestation is defined as "an event, action, or object that clearly shows or embodies something, especially a theory or an abstract idea." We are always manifesting. Each thought we have creates an energy flow within and around our physical beings. This energy attracts its likeness. For example, a high-level thought such as "I rock!" exudes an energy of confidence and in turn attracts great experiences into your life. Each thought you have informs your energy, and your energy manifests into your experiences. Your thoughts and energy create your reality.

This ingredient is vital because you have to create the energy for that which you ask for and wish to receive. You have to become the magnet to attract. If you want a million dollars, you have to create a frequency and a vibe that draws you to that vehicle that will take you to where your million dollars is. If you want a promotion, you will have to play the part of that executive long before you get the office. I used to hear people say, "Dress how you want to be addressed." The way you enter the room is the energy you will receive in that room. Create the energy you want so you can attract greatness.

Also, you must be intentional on your manifestation. Your intentions create your reality. A course I took with Shanel Cooper-Sykes showed us that, on some level, you've asked for everything that happens in your life. How you show up. How you manifest. Your energy is why you are in the place you're in presently. Remember, like attracts like. Therefore, you must be clear on what you do and have a purpose behind it, because what you manifest in the moment of intentional movement will ultimately be your end result.

Since manifesting is the magnet that will begin the attracting process, here are five tips on manifesting your desires.

Clear Space

Before you begin the manifestation process, you must take the necessary time to release all disbelief in your power to be happy. One of the best ways to clear the blocks of doubt is to pray for release. Your job in this step is to pray for guidance to remove all that blocks you from believing in your greatness. Then, allow the universe to help guide you to whatever assignments you need to aid in the healing process. Show up for the assignments and trust that the more you clean your thoughts and energy, the more positive experiences you will attract into your life.

Get Clear

Clarity is king when it comes to manifesting your desires. You must have clear intentions for what you want to call in. Otherwise, you will manifest a lot of what you don't want. Focus on what you desire and then make a list of all that goes along with it.

The most important part of this step is to clarify how you want to feel. When you get clear on how you want to feel, you can begin to access that feeling. That feeling is what makes the manifestation come into form.

Think It, Feel It, Believe It!

Take your clear intention and spend time every day sitting in the feeling of what it is that you desire. You might access the feeling through meditation and visioning exercises, or you may call on the feeling when you're in nature or doing a form of exercise that you love. From a metaphysical perspective, if you believe it, then it is already here. So, make time for contemplating, thinking, feeling, and believing.

Chill!

The next step is crucial to the manifestation process. To truly manifest your desires into form, you gotta chill out! Trust that God has a much better plan than you do. Though you are clear about what you want, you cannot control the timing or the form in which it comes. Stay calm, relax, and trust that the universe has your back!

Know That God Has Your Back

When you're in the know, you're deliberate about what you want. When you're in the know, you no longer vibrate energy of fear or disbelief. When you diligently practice steps one through four, you will clean house, get clear, and feel happier. Accepting your greatness at this moment, right now, is what manifests more greatness. Being in the know helps you recognize that you're already living in your desired manifestation. When you feel it, you live it—regardless of what is happening on the outside.

Patience

Along with manifestation, patience is everything in this process. Nothing you want—at least anything with great substance and longevity—will be created overnight. Let's say that again. Nothing you want—at least anything with great substance and longevity—will be created overnight. Got it! Plus, you have more work to do before you are even in the right position to receive it. I often tell my coaching clients, "You must be in alignment with what you seek and grateful for what you already have before given anything else." If you're the type of person who complains about wanting more without taking moments to enjoy and thank God for what you already have, why would you be granted any request? I have seen people complain day in and day out, never once uttering thanks for being blessed with waking up that day. Complaining and whining are all they seem to do. Then they wonder why they have not received a raise, job promotion, good relationship, or financial blessing. Just everything in life is wrong. Remember, you create that. Every time you complain about all that is wrong in your life, it continues to manifest in your reality and keeps you complaining. To flip that, speak winning and greatness in the moment of adversity.

In 2014 on June 3rd, after renting a house from one of my brothers, I was told that I had to move by July 1st because the neighborhood was getting bad. The truth was, I was illegally renting the house. I was technically renting the house from my brother, who was renting the house from the owner. At that moment, I gave up. Fear flooded my mind, and the projection of being unprepared as a mother played with my psyche. I manifested everything wrong. For an entire week, I manifested the spirit of homelessness and nothingness. I had no more fight in me. But, when my mother shared my situation with my aunt and cousin, I used that ounce of hope to manifest us moving to Abington, Pennsylvania. Two weeks later, my aunt allowed my sons and me to move in with them. I moved from Upper Darby, Pennsylvania, to Abington, Pennsylvania, to live in a better and more suburban single home. Do you think I would have received that yes if I was manifesting negativity? Even though I had to sit for a while in the meantime, I had to manifest and wait. It was the longest three weeks ever, but I managed to survive.

I know exercising patience can be hard at times. With living in a society where everything is automatic, convenient, and instant, the trait of patience is fading. People are dying over road rage, fighting in department stores, and cursing out cashiers because they stood in line for five minutes to check out. I had a coaching client tell me, "This millionaire and success stuff must happen now. It's either now or never." Excuse me, sweetie, but what work are you doing to earn a million dollars now? You don't even know your industry yet! Haven't sold ten books! Remember, your life is like a seed. You must plant what you want and wait for the outcome, but in the meantime, use the tools to stay in alignment to receive it once it blossoms.

Environment

Your environment plays on your ability to manifest and practice patience. Who you're connected to and speak to on a daily basis contributes to how you move. What you see helps you manifest or denies you the belief of receiving. The energy around you motivates you to pursue your goals or stops the progress. Your environment and the people within it dictates just how fearful or successful you will become. Right now, I want you to look around wherever you are and take inventory of what you see, hear, and feel. Do you see, hear, or feel anything that is in alignment with your desires? Use the lines below to write down what you see, hear, and feel in your environment.

_____
_____
_____
_____
_____
_____
_____
_____

Now, look at what you wrote. How is this environment adding value to your desires and goals?

_____
_____
_____
_____
_____

_____

_____

_____

Do you think it's time to change some things around you? Can you change the scenery around you by hanging up a new picture or putting a different table cloth on the dining room table? How about putting up an inspirational poster that will motivate you every time you enter the room? While building faith, you have to create the environment you want so it will give you the confidence to know that it's coming. I have found that people tend not to stress when they can see what they want while waiting for it, rather than waiting and not knowing what to expect. Visual images or vision boards can help for those who need a visual. You can add value however you choose, but you have to be able to envision what you want.

Another way to embrace patience in your waiting season is by experiencing what you are about to receive. I often tell my clients, "You will only believe in what you actually experienced in your life." In other words, you will only know to be true what you already experienced. Some people are stuck in their space of life because they haven't experienced anything greater. If you've only eaten chicken, how can you share the taste of lobster with me? You can't! So, you must create new experiences within your life until the experiences become your life. You don't stop living. You have to experience more to have more. The more you expand your environment, network with new people and try life from a different perspective, the faster your seed can grow. But, also, you will be so excited during the waiting season that you will forget the process and walk right into your new life. Remember, you attract what you want.

So, this week, make it a point to do these five things to enjoy the wait and change your experience.

- Who's in your circle? Find a networking event and attend. Who knows, your next boss could be there waiting to offer you a better salary.
- Want a new car? Take a trip to some dealerships and test drive the car of your dreams.
- Need new friends? Join professional or personal groups of your interest and connect with those who you can learn from and who have what you desire.
- Looking for a new house? Attend some open houses so you can get an idea of different houses and the feeling you get when you enter.

Get the point? Whatever it is you want to experience in your environment, go and try it. You'll never know if you like it until you're around it before you own it.

Work

The last but fun part of the "meantime" process is work! Just like when it comes to manifesting, having patience, and creating the right environment, you must work. You can't simply sit, pray, and wait for your faith to evolve into reality. Referring to the Bible, the need for work is written in James 2:17, "Even so faith, if it hath not works, is dead," and 2 Thessalonians 3:10, "For even when we were with you, this we commanded you, that if any would not work, neither should he eat."

Work is the only power that can transform Faith into Reality. Prayer can offer you strength and guidance, but it's work that takes you across the finish line to the win. I remember having a conversation with a church member about this topic, and she believed prayer was enough. I challenged her by asking, "Why are you working? Why are you out here sacrificing your hours in exchange for dollars to make ends meet? Stop working. Then sit, pray, and wait. Tell me how long that lasts." She gave me a look and said, "I have to work to pay my bills. God is not a magician." I replied, "Exactly!"

God requires your effort and help to get it done. Plus, your work is your proof to Him that you want it. If you think or believe the same as that church member, then I am sorry to disappoint you and pray that you continue reading this book. However, as we all know, the truth and the Word can sometimes hurt our egos or lack thereof.

I know you may be asking, *what does this work look like, Charron?* It will seem different for everybody, but I can guarantee it will require you to get in alignment to receive. Whatever you ask for will require you to have completed all of the prerequisites needed for you to understand what's coming. You must also know how to keep it. It's never fun to manifest a car and receive it, only to have it repossessed a year later. So, when it comes to work, you must not only complete the work to receive it but also create backup plans to keep it. For example, if you desire to further your education and have already received your acceptance letter, you might think all you have to do is the work to secure the degree. Nope, there's more. You'll need to make sure you have a financial backup plan to purchase books, supplies, and pay for the courses if you run out of grant or loan money. It is not enough to get the letter; you have to prepare yourself for everything else that might come up during your journey to graduation day. It's a process of work that builds and builds until the end. But, now that you have the degree, you now have to work towards paying back the loans if you took out any. Never-ending, right? Well, this is my reality, but I have embraced the fact that I will die with these loans unless one of these books or plays serve me to the winner's circle, which is something I manifest every day while remaining relevant in the world of arts.

Now, manifest and get clear on the work you need to do. Writing out your to-do list will help you get organized about what you need to do and get focused to get it done. If you are a visual person, this list will serve you well. If you want to be creative with your list, add images so you can see the action you need to take and the result after implementing the actions. It's nothing like seeing the entire picture upfront. Start creating your to-do list here:

_____
_____
_____
_____
_____
_____
_____
_____
_____
_____
_____
_____
_____
_____
_____
_____

HOW TO BREAK THE CHAINS

Many people need help with this. How does one break the chains of fear so they can live in faith and complete freedom? Well, when the spirit of fear invades my conscious mind, I get my bible and read my favorite verses:

- Deuteronomy 31:8 – *He will never leave you nor forsake you. Do not be afraid; do not be discouraged.*
- Romans 8:28 – *And we know that in all things God works for the good of those who love him, who have been called according to his purpose.*
- Isaiah 43:1 – *Don't fear, for I have redeemed you; I have called you by name; you are mine.*

- Psalm 27:1 – *The Lord is my light and my salvation—whom shall I fear?*

Psalm 27 is the chapter my bible remains open to because everything within that chapter speaks on how God and his promise protects you.

Psalm 27

¹ The Lord is my light and my salvation—whom shall I fear? The Lord is the stronghold of my life—of whom shall I be afraid?

² When the wicked advance against me to devour me, it is my enemies and my foes

who will stumble and fall.

³ Though an army besiege me, my heart will not fear; though war break out against me,

even then I will be confident.

⁴ One thing I ask from the Lord, this only do I seek: that I may dwell in the house of the Lord all the days of my life, to gaze on the beauty of the Lord and to seek him in his temple.

⁵ For in the day of trouble he will keep me safe in his dwelling; he will hide me in the shelter of his sacred tent and set me high upon a rock.

⁶ Then my head will be exalted above the enemies who surround me; at his sacred tent I will sacrifice with shouts of joy; I will sing and make music to the Lord.

⁷ Hear my voice when I call, Lord; be merciful to me and answer me.

⁸ My heart says of you, "Seek his face!" Your face, Lord, I will seek.

⁹ Do not hide your face from me, do not turn your servant away in anger; you have been my helper. Do not reject me or forsake me, God my Savior.

¹⁰ Though my father and mother forsake me, the Lord will receive me.

¹¹ Teach me your way, Lord; lead me in a straight path because of my oppressors.

¹² Do not turn me over to the desire of my foes, for false witnesses rise up against me,

spouting malicious accusations.

¹³ I remain confident of this: I will see the goodness of the Lord in the land of the living.

¹⁴ Wait for the Lord; be strong and take heart and wait for the Lord.

When you read these words, don't they resonate with you a sense of "I got this"? If God is for me, who can be against me? David wrote Psalm 27 to encourage himself in the Lord in the midst of the battle. Your fear is nothing more than your internal battle keeping you from your mental and emotional desires. Fear is your subconscious making you question yourself. Questions—such as, "what if," "when this happens, then what," and "are you sure this is something you want to do,"—will have you doubting yourself. But, when you have faith in your Lord and yourself, only then will you be able to win the battles of your conscious. Remember, fear was embedded in your spirit; it was not something you were born with, and it is not hereditary. It's a virus that will suck you dry and leave you feeling lifeless and regretful.

Coaching Moment!

To see how fear has delayed your living, write below what fear has cost you. What did you say "no" to out of fear while deep down wanting to say "yes"? Are you truly living your best life, or are you settling because of the life choices you made? What should you have but don't because of fear?

_____
_____
_____
_____

_____
_____
_____
_____
_____
_____
_____
_____
_____
_____

Now, imagine life without fear. Where would you be? What would you be doing? Who would you have married? Would you be driving the car you have or working at your present job? Imagine life with no fear and only faith. Although some will say this is impossible since nothing is perfect, living a fearless life does not mean you will not experience failures or make mistakes. It means you are permitting yourself to LIVE. Let's do an exercise that I do weekly to keep me on track.

- Close your eyes and see your life with no fear. Sit there for at least five minutes.
- Embrace your feelings. How do you feel? Where are you? What do you see?
- Now open your eyes and…

Write your vision below:

_____
_____
_____
_____
_____
_____
_____
_____
_____
_____
_____

Now, if you gave yourself permission to live fearlessly and without restrictions, everything in your vision should be unattainable for you right now. In the next chapter, I will provide you with steps on how to make your vision a reality without it costing you too much. Warning, it will require you to let go, relocate, quit, say goodbye, and eliminate some things. Before you can walk into your fearless life, you must FIRST remove everything you've settled for.

If you did this correctly, you should feel intimidated and like you can't achieve your vision. If you're not experiencing a feeling of intimidation and doubt, then you are so programmed to fear that you have forgotten how to feel life beyond the confines of your four walls.

This is not necessarily a bad thing; however, now you know just how deeply rooted fear is in your life and how much conscious and subconscious work you have to do. To give you motivation, three women and one male will share their story of overcoming their fear in order to live their best life. This does not mean they no longer have problems, but now, they are living life with no regrets.

The court calls Elizabeth to the stand...

Please state your name and title for the reader:

Greetings! My name is Elizabeth Dionna, and I'm an actress, writer, producer, director, and the founder/CEO of Hummingbird Butterfly Productions, LLC

Please raise your right hand. Do you swear to tell the truth, the whole truth, and nothing but the truth, so help you God?

I do.

Please have a seat and state your case involving fear.

When initially asked to write about how I overcame fear in my life through my faith, I was honored and excited that someone recognized my hard work and sacrifice. As I began thinking of how to articulate my story so someone else could grow from it, I started hearing that all-too-familiar voice that constantly tries to tell us that we can't do something, the voice that says "you're not good enough" or "no one cares what you think." This time, however, I refused to let that voice or anyone else's opinion keep me from my destiny in life. So, I'm writing my story to show that prayer is the only answer to getting past fear. The more you practice talking to God, the better life gets.

Born and raised in Kansas City, Missouri, I always knew I was meant to perform. As a child, I would play for hours acting out scenes from movies and pretending as if I were the director. My mother, Donna L. Birks, who is also my biggest supporter, always lovingly told me, "You've been my little drama queen your entire life, so you are destined to succeed in Hollywood." Holding tight to my dream, my mother's motivation, and most importantly, my faith in God, I mustered up the courage to leave my full-time political career behind and move to California in 2012.

I had no idea how I was going to be successful in the entertainment industry, so I initially found a secure job working in the political field. During which time, I combined my passion for acting with my purpose to serve the community. I wrote, produced, and performed in *Discrimination Diaries*, an original stage play in September 2017 that would bring exposure to

California state legislation intended to combat workplace discrimination. The play was a huge success, and I am currently pitching it for a national tour through my film and theater production company, Hummingbird Butterfly Productions, LLC. This accomplishment showed me that I could be successful in the entertainment industry while simultaneously helping others to progress. Had I not taken the first step towards happiness, I would not have a testimony today.

During the impetus of my acting career, I was suddenly released from my salary job. I lost my financial means while living in one of the most expensive cities in the world. So, I had to downsize and move. After losing my job, I felt depressed, fearful, undeserving, and insecure. I allowed my former employer, the media, and cultural appropriation to make me believe I was not talented, intelligent, or beautiful enough to succeed as an actress. It was a painful transition, and I was not my best self. I was self-loathing, judgmental of myself and others, and even a little mean. I felt my light beginning to dim, but I remembered how prayer and faith had helped me to triumph over the setbacks in life so many times before. I consulted with my mother, and her answer was always the same: PRAY. At first, I was reluctant because I kept trying to figure out what I was supposed to do while waiting on God. The noise of the city told me that I did not have time to pray but that I needed to figure out how to survive on my own, and God would jump in when he's ready. I always laugh at myself when I think about how foolish this sounded.

Again, my mother would ask me, "Are you praying?" So, I kept praying, and before I knew it, everything started to fall into place. I was cast to perform in Charron Monaye's stage play, *Get Out of Your Own Way*, playing the role of Tiffany, one of the lead actresses. The sold-out show is now being considered for an NAACP Image Award and will start on a national tour in 2019. In the same year, I received notification that Jean-Claude La Marre's latest film, *Kinky*, my first feature film starring Vivica Fox, Dawn Richardson, Robert Ri'chard, and Obba Babatundé, would be released in theaters! Now I am directing a stage play for the first time!

It was not until I was released from my salary job that I was able to enthrall myself into the art of acting, which I had always loved so much. I replaced my fear with faith. Instead of letting negativity hold me back, I used this time to reflect on my goals and life's purpose. I worked on developing my craft by training with one of the premier acting coaches, Tasha Smith, at Tasha Smith's actors' workshop. I also exercised mentally and physically, focusing on my mantra "Love &

Justice. Love for God, self, and others, and Justice for All".

Colossians 1:4 says, "For we have heard of your faith in Christ Jesus [the leaning of your entire human personality on Him in absolute trust and confidence in His power, wisdom, and goodness] and of the love which you have and show for all the saints (God's consecrated ones)." I believe in the power of God and know I would not have so many victories in life if it were not for my complete faith in the Lord and my gratitude for the abundance of blessings in my life. To receive all of God's blessings, one must first be prepared and above all else PRAY.

The court calls Toni to the stand...

Please state your name and title for the reader:

Greetings! My name is Toni Moore, and I am a Transformational Business Development Strategist and an attorney.

Please raise your right hand. Do you swear to tell the truth, the whole truth, and nothing but the truth, so help you God?

I do.

Please have a seat and state your case involving fear.

Fear should be charged with the crime of attempted murder. Fear is a liar and deceiver; fear seems so real that it causes a person to wonder why they would question it. Fear has stopped me from doing things many times. I gave up on romantic opportunities, quit jobs that I felt didn't have my back because of their process, and questioned mentors who tried to lead me down a path that most people who looked and talked like me had never taken.

I recall a time in my life when fear tried to detour me from seeking IVF treatment when I learned that scar tissue was blocking the passage from my tubes to my uterus. Fear tried to convince me that the reason I was having difficulties getting pregnant was that I lost my virginity before marriage. When that didn't work, fear tried to convince me that seeking doctors' assistance was sacrilegious because I was trying to replace God's plans for my life. When I pushed through anyway, fear convinced me that my eggs would split so much that I would give birth to malformed triplets. Now that made me pause.

When I began undergoing the procedure, fear wouldn't leave me alone. Instead, it attempted to abort my progress every step I took. Fear magnified my fear of needles, hospitals, rejection, and failure. Everywhere I went, fear followed me so much that I felt as though it was trying to bully me into doing its bidding. I almost gave in to fear through my season of infertility. When I refused to listen to fear, it attempted to entrap me by presenting accomplices to do its bidding.

Fear cunningly supported the statistics when I didn't produce enough eggs during my cycle. Fear mangled the truth so much that it nearly convinced me that my chance of success was abysmal. Fear even convinced a nurse to counsel me about stopping the cycle and restarting again. She was so sweet on the phone and suggested I think over my decision before canceling my cycle.

Fear didn't tell me what could happen if I stayed on the path. Fear denied me envisioning raising a second child with my husband. Instead, fear spoke to me daily. Whenever I researched the possibilities of giving birth to a healthy child, fear would usurp my internet search by directing me to websites that showed the negativity of IVF.

Fear painted a bleak picture of a failed marriage, lack of money, and other less than desirable situations in an attempt to get my body to abort my child from the stress. When fear realized I had made up my mind to press through, fear made it difficult to inject the needles to keep my child in my womb. When I got over my fear of needles, fear made me think I would have triplets that would die during the second trimester. Even when my child was born healthy and strong, fear made me believe he would die of SIDS. If it weren't for hope that whispered into my spirit, I would have missed out on the one opportunity to birth my second child who helped me reconnect with my true self. In light of what fear attempted to steal, kill, and destroy—

my child's life, which restored my spirit—fear should be charged for the crime of attempted murder of my destiny.

The court calls Parenthysis to the stand…

Please state your name and title for the reader:

Greetings my name is Parenthysis E. Gardner, and I am an accomplished scene and playwright, actress, director, singer, poetess, and creative humanitarian.

Please raise your right hand. Do you swear to tell the truth, the whole truth, and nothing but the truth, so help you God?

I do.

Please have a seat and state your case involving fear.

I met the love of my life in a music studio in 1995. No, it wasn't love at first sight, but there was a lot of sparks from the beginning. He was a creator, just like me. We did everything together. We'd write, sing, and listen to each other. His music was part of his legacy. He once told me to make sure the music he created would not be in vain if anything ever happened to him. I supported him as a musician and artist, and he knew how important being a creative thespian meant to me. So, he eagerly supported me, as well. For years, happiness was a thing that flowed smoothly in our lives. We had everything we ever wanted. Love, a great family—both blood and extended. His mom meant the world to me, and she always made me feel like I was the best thing that ever happened to her and her son. We were a beautiful combination of unfailing love. We were following a dream and a purpose that we both shared. We'd talk about buying our mothers their dream houses and making sure they never had to worry about a thing. We talked about having our own family—a junior for him and a beautiful baby girl for me—and creating a dynasty. We experienced the most genuine expressions of love. Things weren't always perfect, but it was just right for us. Then the unforeseen happened.

A knock on the door; that knock everyone dreads to open at three o'clock in the morning. He had an accident and was taken to the hospital. He was still breathing but on life support and unresponsive. A few days later, I watched him take his last breath. I kissed him and whispered in his ear, "I promise I will not let your legacy go in vain as long as your spirit stays with me."

For months, you couldn't tell me he was gone. But, the reality was the piece of my heart that made me complete was broken. The one person who I never thought I would walk this journey without was taken away from me unexpectedly. I tried to keep that promise. I worked harder at the dream we were trying to build. I worked harder on trying to buy those homes for our mothers and to make sure I shared his music with the world. I was doing so well at first!

A few years after his passing, his mother lost her battle with cancer. She always said I was the last thing that connected her to him, but the truth of the matter is, it was the other way around. I lost myself. I lost my smile. I stopped everything that had to do with the arts because it was too painful to do it without him, without them. I became complacent. I fell into the trap of being comfortable with being ordinary, even though I spent so much of my time in the presence of being extraordinary.

My dreams slowly became my nightmares. I gave up on the dream. I no longer had my support team or the passion I once had for the arts. Then, one day, after I got sick and tired of praying and crying, I decided to sit down and write, because for so many years writing is what brought happiness into my life, and I wanted that feeling again. So, I wrote a piece entitled "He Calls Me Rib". It was a piece about the love and endurance of a husband and wife once tragedy unfolds in their lives. The piece was filled with all of the elements that brought us together and the realizations that caused us to part. I released and revealed so much pain in that script. It became my self-proclaimed therapy. I premiered it in Philadelphia in 2012, and even though it flourished, my smile was not the same. I knew I was still on a journey of self-discovery. I needed something more. I couldn't move forward in the space that I was in mentally. Everything and everywhere reminded me of them. I realized that in order to hold on, I had to let go!

April 2013, I decided to let go of everything. I sold everything in my house except for a few clothes and my guitar. I took that script that had now become the prototype to rebuilding my life and moved halfway across California, although I had never explored the state before. I didn't know what was going to happen or where I would end up. I just knew I had to take a risk. I was willing to face anything I had to go through to get my life back, the life that I deserved.

"He Calls Me Rib" was the first sold-out play I produced in California. After that, my life started all over again. The passion I had once lost was slowly returning to its perfect place. I learned that losing someone is never easy. Yes, memories will always allow the heart to remember, and that's perfectly fine.

It's a part of this thing we call life, but we can't let the sorrows in our lives hinder our tomorrows. I guess the lesson was, in order to begin again, some things must end. I still use his music for transition in my scripts and screenplays to celebrate the dreams we shared, but I know that as long as I am breathing, the dream is not over.

Since leaving the past behind, I have directed over fifteen productions and added to my literary catalog. I've toured. I have been featured in a few films. I have won a few awards. I have been recognized as one of the most sought after, up and coming artists on a few media platforms. I am building my network and net worth. But, most of all, I have gotten my smile back, and I'm okay with that!

The court calls Christopher to the stand…

Please state your name and title for the reader:

Greetings my name is Christopher Hopson, and I am an actor and singer, co-founder of Pen Legacy, LLC, and Senior Airman of the Civil Air Patrol. I am also the oldest son to Charron Monaye.

Please raise your right hand. Do you swear to tell the truth, the whole truth, and nothing but the truth, so help you God?

I do.

Please have a seat and state your case involving fear.

Let me start by saying, being the child of Charron Monaye comes with a lot of pressure. From all of the degrees she's earned and her entrepreneurial journey, how could I ever outdo her? She truly set the bar high for my brother and me, but knowing the kind of mother she is, she will help us. Even though she is this major person and people look up to her, she manages to let me and my brother remain individuals and youthful.

My mom's biggest love and drug is education. Education is a priority and the driving force behind the woman you see. My mother has a Bachelor's of Arts in Political Science from West Chester University, a Master's in Public Administration from Keller Graduate School of Management, certificates in Paralegal Studies and Life Coaching, and an Honorary Doctorate in Philosophy. This woman thrives on learning. If she is not taking a coaching class, she is reading a book to learn more or watching some educational or news channel. She loves learning so much she has a wall that has all of her degrees hanging on it, a constant reminder of what we have to achieve to make our mother proud. But how, when school is alright? I'm still trying to figure out why and when I am going to use some of this knowledge in the real world. I mean, some of the classes I took were completely useless, but even in my disagreement, I was challenged with passing it. Thus, requiring me to take an interest, study, and do the homework.

By the time I went into the 10th grade, my mother and I started doubting my life after high school. In her most frustrated voice, my mom told me, "You only have two options: military or college. Anything else will leave you here in the backroom, borrowing money from me, and possibly becoming another statistic. I have worked too hard to watch you fail yourself and your life. So, pick your poison." After hearing that speech and feeling like a failure, I started to think college wasn't for me. So, I went to the Marines recruitment center; my mother and brother came along. While taking the test, something in my mind kept saying, "Military is not your calling." When I finished the test and was informed I had failed, I was excited because I knew I should set my sights on going to college. I just needed to buckle down.

Once I started the 12th grade, it was game time. I took the SAT in October of 2018 and scored higher than my mother. Man, I was excited. However, since my grade point average was low, my mother paid for me to attend Huntington Learning Center for SAT tutoring. I went every Monday for two hours. My mother would take me and pick me up. That alone let me know she wanted me to succeed just as much as I wanted to. So, I gave it my all, making sure not to waste her investment or my time. Plus, I had schools that I applied to, so achieving a higher score was necessary.

Each week that I attended tutoring, I would think to myself, *You have to get one thousand or higher on this test. No military for me.* Plus, I didn't take joy in seeing my mother push herself by working all day, then getting dinner—whether cooking or ordering us food, driving to the learning center, going back home, driving back to get me once I was finished, and driving back home once more. Some days, she would be so exhausted that once she walked through the door, she would immediately crash on her bed. I felt so bad, because if I would have taken school more seriously, my mother wouldn't have been going non-stop from six-thirty in the morning until eight-thirty at night, or even later.

When I took the test in December, I put my future on the paper so my mother could be proud. For a woman who has been there for us, sacrificed sleep and sometimes eating, and committed herself to her children, the most we can do as her children is to bring home good grades. For years, I feared I could never match my mother's greatness, but once I grew up, I learned that education is why she is great! So, to match my mother, I needed to get serious.

On December 14, 2018, my mother got an email saying I was accepted into Prairie View A & M. Then she received another email saying I got the score I needed on my SAT. I did it! College, here I come! Even though I feared not making it here, I made it and with my mother by my side. With everything she has taught my brother and me, her teaching us that success is nothing without sacrifice has turned out to be the realest advice. For years, I have watched her struggle and sacrifice, but look at her now. I faced my fear of not matching my mother, and even with this little victory, I am proud and can't wait to put my degree on her wall.

Thank you, Mommy, for everything you have done. I may not surpass your legacy, but I am going to create one that will truly match your gangsta!

When you remove fear, you give yourself permission to live. There is a mantra that I live by: *Life gives you a birth date and a death date, but the true test of life is what you do in between.* What are you doing in between that will keep your footprints in the sand of the generations to come? How will your legacy be remembered? How accomplished are you and how much success have you achieved in your life? How much is your inheritance worth? Will the future generations of your family be able to cash in on your comfortability?

For this last exercise, I want you to write your obituary. An obituary is not a biography but a recount of important events, qualities, contributions, and connections in a person's life. I want you to see just how your life—as it is right now with fear and limitations—will be remembered. If you have never written an obituary, here are the steps:
- Begin with the name, age, and place of residence of the deceased, along with the time and place of death.
- List events chronologically, putting the deceased's accomplishments, marriage, children born, education, etc. Mention significant contributions and recognition.
- Incorporate involvement in service and social organizations, hobbies, places of employment, and places of residence.

- List survivors and those who preceded the loved one in death.

Easy enough? Below, write out your obituary as it stands today. For some, this will be quite difficult. For others, it should be a breeze. Whatever your outcome is, please know that whatever you're lacking won't come until fear is released.

_____
_____
_____
_____
_____
_____
_____
_____
_____
_____
_____
_____
_____
_____
_____
_____
_____
_____

FACE EVERYTHING AND RISE

When I first saw the acronym F.E.A.R., I thought to myself, *How is this impossible?* Then I sat back and ignored it. Years later, I was challenged by God to complete a dream that I once had five years earlier. In 2012, I threw my pen in the playwright ring and tried my luck with stage plays. Before that, I had authored and released my first book, *My Side of the Story*, and was still an amateur in this entrepreneur business. I was overcoming a divorce and trying to rebuild my life as a single mother. In my spare time, I religiously watched Tyler Perry's play, *I Can Do Bad All by Myself*. The storyline was amazing, and the actors were personal journeys spoken to me. Most importantly, it resonated with my situation; I was by myself.

Checking my bank account and seeing there was only $3.19 in it, and knowing my rent that was $725.00 was due in two days, I had to think of a plan. I had my book that was selling, but what else could I do to earn money? Then it clicked. *You can write a play!* Now mind you, I am no playwright, formally or informally. My educational background is in law and government. I have no formal training as a writer, so why I thought I could be a playwright was beyond me. However, I dared to be great, so Google became my friend. I looked up scripts and learned and penned my first script, *Living Your Life*. This play would later premiere September 26, 2012, in Philadelphia, Pennsylvania, and even though I walked away broke, it was something about the audience's reaction that made me embrace theater. As an author, you have to wait to read reviews to know if people either liked or disliked your book, but as a playwright, you hear their feedback throughout the whole show. After this, I started writing scripts and more scripts until I had no more dialogue in me. Then, in 2013, I penned the script, *Get Out of Your Own Way*.

Very great play, but God gave me the assignment to release it in California. I knew nobody in California, and I lived in Philadelphia. What was I going to do, allow fear of the unknown stop me? No, I proceeded and tried to build a team from the resources that I knew, who knew people in California and went on with my show. I found a director, and he cast the show. A flyer was created, and it was time for me to start producing. But then, either fear or God stepped in, and I canceled the show. Made one call and that was over.

What to do now? Back to writing books I went and kept writing until 2017 when I got a nudge to try again. Remembering what I went through in 2013, fear stepped in and shut it down. Two weeks later, another nudge. This time, I said an encouragement prayer that I learned from my coach, Iyanla Vanzant, and called an actress who was in my first play—but who had moved to California—to see what we could do together. She read the script and agreed to direct. Then I started hearing the naysayers:

- Why are you producing a play over there? No one is going to show up.
- That's going to be a waste of money.
- Nobody knows you over there.
- Are you even a playwright? When was your last play?

I heard it all! And just like in 2013, I was ready to call and cancel it. At the same time, I wanted to prove to myself that I could face this challenge of producing a play while being 2,716.9 miles away, which was equivalent to forty hours of driving time. Who was I fooling, though? The only person I knew over there was my director. Instead of second-guessing myself, I rose to the occasion and promoted my behind off as if my life depended on it. I knew people were watching and waiting for me to fail or for me to cancel it. But, I used every resource and entrepreneur strategy I knew to get money to pay for the play and to fly over there, with my children, to see it premier. Not only did I produce the play with no stress, but I also walked away with three sold-out shows, profit, and a tour schedule (with a producer attached).

PenLegacy Presents
OCT 5TH – 7TH, 2018

When Death Meets Secrets

Marwan Granville · Sunshine Parkman · Chantal Sidney · Randahl Ginyard · Cer Brisco · Elizabeth Collins Dionna

Tyrone Dubose · Saundra Charleston

GET OUT OF YOUR OWN WAY
THE COMPLEX THEATER ON SANTA MONICA IN HOLLYWOOD CA 90038

WRITTEN AND PRODUCED BY Charron Monaye DIRECTED BY Parenthysis E. Gardner
PRODUCTION ASSISTANT Sharon Judie RED CARPET HOST Madison Jaye HOSTED BY Robert Grant

GET OUT OF YOUR OWN WAY (TOUR)

Tiffany's Place

WHEN DEATH MEETS SECRETS

Shaunte • Apollo • Sidney • Elizabeth • Cer • Jessica

Tour Dates

Hollywood, CA - Jan 19, 2019
Charlotte NC - March 23, 2019
Cleveland OH - April 20, 2019
New York, NY - May 11, 2019
Killeen TX - July 20, 2019

WRITTEN BY
CHARRON MONAYE

DIRECTED BY
PARENTHYSIS E. GARDNER

PRODUCTION ASSISTANT
SHARON Y. JUDIE

PRODUCED BY
TYRONE CHANDLER

Showtimes: 3pm & 7pm
For Ticket Info & Locations
www.charronmonaye.com/events

I faced my fear and used it to motivate me to excel all expectations. I went in as the underdog and came out the winner. I know you're thinking, *That is amazing, Charron, but how do I achieve that?* Well, I have an answer, and in this chapter, I will help you achieve what you envision and make whatever you want to come true a reality. How I'll do that is by giving each letter of the word FEAR an actionable meaning, which will provide you with practical instructions to move you from Existing to Living.

FACE

Just like the exercise we did in the previous chapter, you have to face what is wrong—or could be better—in your life in order to give it a new direction. You can't change anything if you don't examine or acknowledge it first. So, facing your life head-on is the first step to changing your mindset of fear. Addressing the "why" helps set the tone on the "what" and gives you the understanding of "how". For example, one of the biggest things I had to face was my commitment to being a people pleaser; that was my "what". I swear, I lived my life concerned with what people perceived about me. My self-worth was so low that I often felt like I was only living to do the work of others, instead of embracing the desires of my heart.

I did not believe I could validate my legacy, because what did I know about life? Even though I had degrees and a government job, I felt like a failure seventy-five percent of the time, and my dad often reminded me. But, it was time to start facing my truth and believing in myself to change that. After facing my truth, I had to believe that what I wanted was mine for the keeping. In that believing, I had to live as if what I wanted was already in my possession. I had to believe I was already successful and award-winning before I actually achieved it and received the titles. You see! When you position yourself with what you want, your behavior, attitude, and energy tend to focus on having it. It's almost like a magnet. When you position one magnet across from another, they are eventually drawn to each other by the force between them. That is how powerful your force should be to have what you want. In your daily life, you should be so focused and energetic that when you step outside your house, your neighbor wants to have a conversation.

To help you get in alignment with this concept, answer the following few questions honestly. Once completed, re-read your answers and make a list of things you need to face and how you plan to reposition yourself.

Coaching Moment!

When you look at your life, how are you living it? (Perspective)

_____
_____
_____
_____
_____
_____
_____
_____
_____

How are you showing up in life?

_____
_____
_____
_____
_____
_____
_____
_____

What is my worth?

_____
_____
_____

How am I being intentional and applying my use of thoughts, words, and feelings?

What is my secret power? Do I use it to my advantage?

After reading these questions, ask yourself, "Am I playing it small?"

Next step, I want to challenge you to write down ten ways you will reposition yourself to gain what you want.

1. _____

2. _____

3. _____

4. _____

5. _____

6. _____

7. _____

8. _____

9. _____

EVERYTHING

Now that you have faced your fears and are setting up your position, let's address the stuff that is hindering you. The letter 'E' should be your breakthrough simply because it's unloading time. When you remove all of the baggage from your life, what do you think will happen? FREEDOM! FAVOR! Weight lifted off of you, making this journey easier. But, before we move any further, let's get clear about our hindrances. I won't ask that you write them down, but I will list some of the common issues I hear from my coaching clients:

- Income – *I don't get paid until next Friday.*
- Guidance – *I want to be rich, but I don't know how.*
- Support – *I don't have anyone in my corner.*
- Enthusiasm – *I'm interested, but I don't care either way.*
- Procrastination – *I'll get to it when I can.*
- Fear of Failure – *I don't want the judgement if this doesn't work.*
- Lack of Goal Setting – *I want to write a book but have no plan in place to execute.*
- Impatient – *My dreams/desires must happen tomorrow, or I'll quit.*
- Self-Sabotaging – *Why do I even bother? It won't work.*
- Unrealistic Expectations – *I want to be debt free in thirty days, but I still use my credit cards.*

- Failure of the Unknown – *If you can't tell me what will happen and how, I can't be bothered.*

If I missed any, please add to the list because I am sure there are more.

When facing change or anything that is outside of your comfort zone, a person will come up with a ton of reasons why they can't do something. I call this the list of excuses, because they are personal choices we make to either accept, achieve, or delay our wrong circumstances. Now, for the sake of what I hear often, I am going to use this section to help with personal finances. For you to face everything and rise, you need money. Money and debt are two of the most important aspects when it comes to living your dream life, but they are also the main issues that stop a lot of people.

Learn how to CREATE, MANAGE, and MULTIPLY MONEY. Some people only understand money in the form of a paycheck every other Friday. But, what if I told you that money, just like anything else, has a process that will either help you or hurt you. When it comes to money, you have to know how to successfully:

Create Money. Sorry to disappoint you, but there are other ways to make money than getting a paycheck. Did you know there are three types of income?

Earned income requires your time. This is the income you receive from actively working. You work and in return are paid for your work.

- Types
  - Employment
  - Small Business
  - Consulting
  - Gambling (Yes, even gambling!)

Portfolio income is money you receive from selling an investment for more than what you paid for it. Portfolio income is also referred to as capital gains.

- Types:
  - Stocks, Bonds, Mutual Funds
  - Stock Market Investing
  - Buying and Selling Real Estate
  - Buying and Selling of Assets

Passive income is money generated from assets you own and doesn't require you to actively work. Passive income is thought to be the key to building wealth. Once you have an investment that generates recurring income, you don't have to do much to maintain it.

- Types:
  - Interest & Dividends
  - Capital Gains

- Royalties
- Rental Income
- Business Income

Manage Money. Now that you have the money, what will you do with it? This is where your choices come into play. For many of us, we were not taught how to manage money. If you were like me, you saw your parents make money, use credit cards, and pay bills. There was no managing or multiplying money; they merely transferred dollars from one account to another to give it away. It was like a funnel that never shut off. So, with witnessing for so many years the way they handled money, how do you reposition your mindset to learn how to manage money? And by managing, I mean paying your expenses and having money left over to save, invest, and enjoy life. You can't live beyond your fears if you have no money. This is why making and managing money is so important.

I listened to a wealth course by David Imonitie, and David dropped some gems on money and how we must change our mindset regarding it. He started by saying, *"Money is not what you want! What you want is what money can do for you."* I thought this statement was powerful because money is the gatekeeper for your dreams. For you to unleash what you desire, you need money. That's why it's crucial for you to reprogram your mind to see money as more than something used to pay your bills. You have to set intentional goals and stick to them. Some sacrificing and rewiring may be required, but I promise you, if you manage money the right way, money will be the least of your worries.

In addition, credit cards are the enemy! Sorry but not sorry. On top of not having enough money, debt is the other reason you have no money. Between the fees and interest rates, some people can barely pay the principle. Some use credit cards as a way to live life. I cringe every time I hear of or see people using a credit card as if it's a debit card. Credit is nothing more than a loan that requires you to pay extra to use it, not unless you can pay the balance off in full before the next billing cycle. So, whenever you mismanagement credit cards, you mess up your whole financial picture, leaving you living under your means and requiring you to use more credit or borrow money from friends.

You can't break fear while living your life in credit card debt. Fear or no fear, you can't face anything if you are dodging creditors.

Multiply Money. Multiplying the money you have to create more money is what keeps you in the game. For those who have a portfolio and passive income, this is easy. However, if you only have earned income, multiplying may be difficult. When it comes to multiplying money, you have to understand the power of taking money and doubling, tripling, etc. You should be able to get a hundred dollars and know how to flip it into a thousand dollars. This step requires personal coaching, because in order to successfully flip money, you must know your gamble, sacrifice, and the exact steps you need to execute with rewards.

For the sake of general learning, I will offer you three easy ways to multiply your money.

- **Spend Less Than You Earn** – Spend less than you earn by investing those savings into an index fund that tracks the S&P 500 and reinvesting your gains.
- **Invest in Bonds** – If your bonds return 5% on average every year, then according to the Rule of 72, you will be able to double your money every 14.4 years.
- **Take Advantage of Your Employer Match** – If your employer matches the contributions into your 401(k), you have the easiest, most risk-free method of doubling your money available at your disposal. For every dollar that you put in, you will get an automatic increase due to employer matching.

ACCOUNTABILITY

Instead of using the word "and" in the acronym F.E.A.R., we are going to use the "a" to cover accountability. According to the dictionary, the definition of accountability is "the fact or condition of being accountable; responsibility." When facing fear, you have to be accountable for your choices (why you're doing it) and actions (how you're doing it). Some people go about living life without well-thought-out decisions, thus causing them to make bad choices and take dumb actions that will only come back to haunt them. As you remove fear, a lot of options and opportunities will present themselves to you, but the thing we often overlook is the thought process behind it all. Before I invest in anything, I first figure out the intention and then the motive. Now, this just may be me being cautious, but I am no fool to what I have to offer or what someone wants from me. By having that understanding, I give permit myself to think before I react, making myself fully responsible for the outcome.

The worst thing you can do when combating fear and living out loud is not having one hundred percent control over your thoughts, actions, feelings, and emotions. Having control of those things makes the change easier to handle and the lesson easier to overcome. Most people use this level to prematurely celebrate the journey without making sure they are prepared, positioned, and freed from baggage. This is where you find disappointment, failure, and setbacks. Not because your request is not for you, but because you did not accept responsibility for EVERYTHING that comes with it. Comedian and Actor Kevin Hart often says, "Everybody wants to be famous, but nobody wants to do the work." This is the work! This is where you apply what you know and prepare for takeoff. This is where you get clear and move on your prayers and faith. This is where you make the hard choices for yourself so you can live for you and be happy. This is where the fun starts, but to get here, you must first face your reality and eliminate your baggage so you can finally walk clearly into your vision.

If you did the work throughout this book, you should be anxious about what's to come. Let me warn you, though. It's also during this step that you can easily be distracted and deterred from your "rise". So how do you stay on track and accountable?

Even as an employee and a mother, I have to remain true to my goals. It is easy to max out my credit cards when they have available balances. I can easily go back to hanging out with friends who rather talk about guys and their problems instead of investing in stocks and retirement plans. Your commitment to your journey is challenging, and sometimes the second-guessing and temptation will come into play when what you want doesn't come fast enough or because you can't go out and splurge on a two-thousand-dollar Louboutin bag. You have to be able to chin-check yourself and remain obedient. Fear can come into play if you have naysayers who will try and talk you out of your goals, like the people who questioned my goal of producing a play in Hollywood. But then, you have to ask yourself is it fear or just hate. If you prepared, planned, prayed for guidance, and have a coach or mentor to work with you, why are you bothered by what others may say?

Knowing firsthand how hard accountability is, here are some strategic ways you can hold yourself accountable and finally receive the life you want:

- Write everything down.
- Identify your mission statement.
- Reward your accomplishments and milestones.
- Create micro-goals.
- Review your performance.
- Seek feedback but remain comfortable with your decision.

RISE

This should be the moment you have been waiting for! It's time to taste and see what you've been dreaming about. Even though the life you want will not fall out of the sky today, you should feel lighter, more equipped, and mentally prepared to go out and get it. You should have a savings account, stable support behind you, and resonating faith. This is the milestone that confirms Psalm 27 and reminds you that there is nothing you and God can't do together. I often tell people that God and I have a personal relationship and partnership. He handles the conditions of the journey, and I do the work to keep the journey alive. Both entities are required to keep the ball rolling. I can't pray for what I want, then sit and wait for God to do it. He is a spirit of faith, not a magician. He requires your teamwork and for you to remain obedient to His calling.

If you followed this F.E.A.R. process, you should be celebrating something or just excited with the thought of knowing how to Face Everything And (Accountability) and Rise! For me, this how-to is a stress reliever. Since everyone's "rise" will be different, I want you to write a celebratory letter to yourself and give yourself a pat on your back for a job well done!

_____

_____

_____

_____

_____

_____

_____

SET THE INTENTION

By the time you have reached this chapter, I pray you have made the conscious decision to take back the power you allocated to others and step into your authentic lane. I pray I have given you some fundamental gems that you will be able to use to build the foundation that will lead to the new and improved you. While you were reading, I hope you noticed that I did not ask of you anything that I did not first ask of myself. I have always found that lessons are best explained to others by those who have lived through and learned from them. Each lesson that I have shared with you, I have already tested in my personal life. I've learned so much from many who have shared their experiences and the lessons they learned from those experiences. Something is moving about hearing a message in one's testimony. I am hoping my learned lessons will help at least one person to avoid the mistakes I made and help them grow. This is what motivates me to share my story.

My ability to be transparent allows me to be an inspiration to others, as well as myself. I use my story and my successes as a means to coach someone else to theirs. I am that vessel that will happily tell you what I did, how I did it, and encourage you to believe that you can do it, too. There is nothing I have in my life that you can't yourself obtain. From my dreams to my freedom, you have the ability to accomplish similar things, and the first step towards achieving this is to own your life.

When I stopped living my life for others and realized my purpose, I started living without apology. I still say "I'm sorry" if I hurt someone's feelings, but I am no longer sorry for who I was or who I was trying to become. I am no longer ashamed of what I want or how I go about getting what I want. I set my standards and play by my own rules in order to live according to my OWN purpose. After fifteen years of living a lie, I can now admit that I've built the strongest and boldest platform upon which to build my future. My new strength is resilient and fearless. All of the hell and turmoil that I was able to overcome has brought me to the place I'm in today, and I desire the same for you.

As I have said in almost every chapter, YOU DESERVE IT! Do you want better? Go get it! I often tell people that the fastest way to get to your dream is by living like you are already in it. I hope you will use this book as a tool to prepare you for your ultimate breakthrough. I want you to join me on the other side of the rainbow, but I need you to cleanse your life and eliminate your baggage in order for you to get there. It's time for you to clean house and fix your life so you can be a part of the successes. Again, I am not telling you anything that I have not already done. I did the work, read the books, organized my life, created the budget, and gave everything a place, leaving me with nothing more to do than enjoy the fruits of it all. Working paycheck to paycheck is sustainable, but working and not having to wait for a payday is less stressful and more rewarding.

How would you like it if you were able to fire your boss and became the CEO of your dreams? How awesome would it be if you could leave your unsupportive mate/spouse and find a person who not only wants to support you but also vows to invest in YOU? All of this is possible if you believe you are worthy of it. Any of this is possible if you eliminate those things or people which hinder you from completing your goals. Saying goodbye to the norm may be difficult, but saying hello to the extraordinary is beyond breathtaking. When you own your life, you own your legacy, and that, my friend, is what others will remember you by. If you do not wish to be remembered as the person that you are, in the place in which you are right now, then allow that to be the motivation to get started on your transformation, if you haven't already started.

What is your intention for your life? What is your specific purpose for living your life? Are you living in it right now? If not, then list below what you will permanently change from this day forward to change your perception about owning your life:

1. _____
   _____
2. _____
   _____
3. _____
   _____
4. _____
   _____

I hope the things you listed are attainable and realistic. Remember, when setting goals, be truthful about your limitations, honest about the things you're willing to do, and then commit to seeing these things through to the end. Your journey is not anyone else's. It is solely yours and must be traversed in a way that will allow you to accept what is beyond your control. Your journey should be outlined according to what you can endure. We all have our own way of achieving success and moving forward to our happiness. My only goal is that you will find that pot of gold at the end of your rainbow. I am in the business of inspiring individuals to be the greatest champions they can be while living on this thing called Earth. The iconic entertainer Prince said it best with his lyrics: *Dearly beloved, we are gathered here today to get through this thing called Life.* That's all any of us are trying to do, get through this thing called Life. So, let's run this race, and let's go crazy together at the finish line! What impacts one will affect another, so we will allow our successes—and even our failures—to elevate our lives overall. Remember, people make the world go 'round, and I want to ensure we are all being touched with positive karma daily.

So, to circle back to the topic at hand, what is your intention now that you have another perspective on living an abundant and authentic life? What will you do with the information given? Will you use my real-life examples and apply the lessons from those examples to better your life? Will you take living seriously and get started on pursuing your dreams?

What will you do now that you know better?

VERDICT

Knowing what we know now about fear, I am going to challenge you to write your verdict for fear and its place in your life moving forward. As you completed the coaching questions and mindset shift challenges, I hope you gained enough information about your introduction to, handling of, and how much access you've given fear in your life. I agree that the "unknown" is intimidating for many of us, but if you trust and believe in yourself enough to know that you will survive no matter what, nothing should be able to stop you. Where is your faith? Don't you know that every time you say "no" to your gift, assignment, calling, or promotion, you are declining your God's blessings. Then, we get mad at God because he won't reissue the opportunities we previously denied because we were complacent.

Face Everything And Rise is how we must overcome the ills of fear! Sometimes to get different results, we have to change the meaning or give it an acronym. I chose to face fear by preparing, planning, praying, executing, and praising while going after what I want. When you follow this formula, you fully position yourself to win.

Mindset Shift Challenge

You didn't think I was going to let you decide the verdict without one more mindset shift, did you? To convict fear and break free from its bondage, we must get a strategy in place to eliminate any room for error. Before we go into this exercise, I want to offer you this prayer by my coach Iyanla Vanzant that I pray. Use it to help you remain in the right space as you get clear on your journey.

Prayer by Iyanla Vanzant

I acknowledge You, God, as my ever-present Source of life and love. I acknowledge Your presence within me. With You and in You, I know I am never alone. I ask to feel Your love flowing into and through me in this moment. I ask for and open myself to be healed from all thoughts, feelings, beliefs and behaviors related to fear. I ask that every memory, fear, and expectation be cleansed and released from my mind, my heart and my soul. Acknowledging You as my constant friend and companion, I ask that every person whom I believe has ever denied me be surrounded and blessed by the pure light of Your presence in my mind.

I ask that any hurt and all wounds caused by the experiences I have named "fear" be filled with the presence of Your love so that they will be healed. Remind me, God, that You love me. Allow me to remember that You are always with me. Fill the empty places in my mind and heart with the fullness of Your grace so that I will know how to and when to let go. I now proclaim my total and complete healing. I call forth situations and circumstances that allow me to know and feel love. I am deeply and profoundly grateful for the power and grace of love present within me and for me. I release the power of these words, knowing that as I let go and let God, it is done. And so it is! Amen.

Where Do I Need Help? Exercise

Look at your life right now. Now use the chart below to rate each area (1 - disagree, 5 -agree). Add up each area. For the areas that have the lowest scores, proceed to the next exercise.

	I have everything I what and need.	I lose sleep over it every night.	Everything I want, I make it happen. I live on Faith.	Total
Spiritual				
Financial				
Physical				
Mental				
Emotional				
Family				
Love				
Dreams				

Face Everything And Rise! Exercise

For this exercise, take the areas with scores lower than 40, and let's use the F.E.A.R. formula to create a new narrative and increase your scores. The happiest life is one that is fully balanced and well-lived. So, take each area and strategize a new plan. Identify what you will need to prepare, read the prayer by Iyanla Vanzant, and give yourself a deadline to accomplish. Then email me at info@penlegacy.com so we can praise and celebrate together. You don't have to do this alone, but you do have to write the blueprint giving yourself clear instructions on what's next and how to finish.

Area #1: _____

What's the plan to achieve?

_____
_____
_____
_____
_____
_____
_____
_____
_____

What do you need to prepare?

_____
_____
_____
_____
_____
_____
_____
_____
_____

Execute with Regulations:

- Deadline?
  _____
- Budget?
  _____
- Is a team necessary?
  _____

What's the final result?

_____
_____
_____
_____
_____
_____
_____

Area #2: _____

What's the plan to achieve?

_____
_____
_____
_____
_____
_____
_____

What do you need to prepare?

_____
_____
_____
_____
_____
_____
_____
_____

Execute with Regulations:

- Deadline?
  _____
- Budget?
  _____
- Is a team necessary?
  _____

What's the final result?

_____
_____
_____
_____
_____
_____
_____
_____

Area #3: _____

What's the plan to achieve?

_____
_____
_____
_____
_____
_____

_____
_____
_____

What do you need to prepare?

_____
_____
_____
_____
_____
_____
_____

Execute with Regulations:

- Deadline?
  _____
- Budget?
  _____
- Is a team necessary?
  _____

What's the final result?

_____
_____
_____
_____

MISSION ACCOMPLISHED

This book teaches you to observe your ways of thinking and to challenge your limiting, non-supportive thoughts, habits, and actions in regards to fear. The reason we start with fear is because it's one of the biggest causes of pain in most people's lives. But, there's a bigger picture to consider. You see, once you start recognizing your non-supportive ways around fear, this awareness will transfer into every other part of your life.

The goal of this book has been to assist you in raising your consciousness. Again, consciousness is observing your thoughts and actions so you can operate from your present choices rather than acting on past programming. It is about the power to respond from your higher self rather than reacting from your fear-based, "lower" self. In this way, you can be the best you can be and fulfill your destiny. But, you know what? The essence of this transformation is not just about you. It is about the entire world. Our world is nothing more than a reflection of the people who make it up. As individuals raise their consciousness, the world increases its consciousness—moving from fear to courage, from hatred to love, and from scarcity to prosperity for all. It is therefore up to each of us to enlighten ourselves so that we may add more light to the world.

If you want the world to be a certain way, then start with being that way yourself. If you want the world to be a better place, start with being a better you. That is why I believe it's your duty to grow yourself to your fullest potential, to create abundance and success in your life; for in doing so, you will be able to help others and positively add to the world. Therefore, I ask you to share this message of consciousness and empowerment with others. Get the message of this book out to as many people as possible. Commit to telling at least one hundred of your friends, family, and associates about it, or consider getting it for them as a life-changing gift. Not only will they be introduced to powerful life-changing concepts, but they will also learn to observe the way they think, raise their consciousness, and in turn, raise the consciousness of the planet. Thank you for reading, and I can't wait to meet you on the other side of your breakthrough.

BONUS:
7 Ways to Get Out of YOUR Own Way!

I hope you enjoyed this book and are more inspired to GO FOR IT! I want to thank witnesses Toni Moore, Esq., Elizabeth Dionna, Parenthysis E. Gardner, and Christopher Hopson for sharing their fear-to-success stories. We all have the opportunity to start again if we want it, and we are dedicated to helping you get out of your own way so you can live an unapologetic life. None of us had it easy, and all of us are still battling issues of insecurities and fears. However, the one thing we have mastered is living in our truth.

Removing fear is no easy task. With all of the self-sabotaging words we embed in our minds and the projections we place on ourselves, we live every day being our worst critic. Can I share a secret with you? No opportunity will ever come if you believe you are not worthy of receiving it or that it's too good to be true. And guess what? You got it! You can handle this!

Now I'm not saying you won't ever experience any fear or doubt, but as long as you are prepared for the ready, equipped with your spirit, and guided by your desires, you will be okay. You can say anything you want about these co-authors, but the one thing you will never be able to say is that they QUIT! I pray others will be able to say the same about you.

Below are seven practical ways you can get out of your own way. Overcoming fear starts with YOU, and as a coach, I feel it is necessary to leave you with actionable tools that will help you further achieve greatness. I can't wait to meet you at the top!

1. Just pull the trigger.
There will always be a reason why you shouldn't do something. What's the trick to overcoming pessimism? Just start. Push through the insecurity that's stopping you. Because once you start, your momentum does, too, and you'll roll right past any obstacles you were anxious about before you started.

2. Do one thing at a time.
If you are like me, you think you can do it all. But, if we're honest with each other, we can't—at least not all at once. It isn't faster to juggle more; it's faster to focus on one thing and then move on to the next. Just like the domino effect, your "row" of to-do's will fall one after the other—one domino at a time.

3. Forget failure.
You can't have success without failure. Yeah, yeah, I know. You've heard it before. So why do we worry about failing when we know it's a necessary part of the process? Do your best to expect failure, and try even harder to learn from it.

4. Be consistent.
Consistency will keep you going. Unfailing hard work will help maintain the momentum you created by first pulling the trigger. "We are what we repeatedly do," Aristotle once said. "Excellence, then, is not an act, but a habit."

5. Choose your friends wisely.
You know the saying "you are what you eat." Well, it's also true when it comes to the company you keep. Are you running with the right crowd? The people you interact with on a daily basis directly influence who you are and what you do. Make sure you surround yourself with people who encourage you and hold you accountable—people who you can teach you positive habits.

6. Systematize everything.
On average, an adult makes roughly 35,000 decisions a day. No wonder we stall out when it comes to getting started on our goals. Systematizing your processes

takes decision-making out of the process, leaving more mental room for bigger and better thinking.

7. Reflect on your influence.
Ask yourself how the work you do affects others. We all transform other people whether we're conscious of it or not. So, for a little motivation, think about how you'll be helping someone else. You starting work on your goal or project could spur someone else to pull the trigger on theirs. You just have to pull your trigger first.

COACHING RESOURCES

6 Money Tips for a Wealthy Life!

- Money tip #1: Eliminate your debt
- Money tip #2: Invest in a 401k
- Money tip #3: Invest in a Roth IRA
- Money tip #4: Automate your finances
- Money tip #5: Leverage sub-savings accounts
- Money tip #6: Use target-date funds

10 Ways To Get Out of Debt

It's amazing that it's so easy (and often fun) to get into debt, but painfully difficult to get back out. It can take just a few months to create tens of thousands of dollars in debt, but sometimes decades to pay it off. Everyone who pays off their debt does it a different way and often combine strategies to knock out bad debt. Here are some ways to get out of debt.

- Stop Creating More Debt
- Increase Your Monthly Payment
- Build an Emergency Fund
- Pick One Debt and Give It All You've Got
- Ask Your Creditor for a Lower Interest Rate
- Look for Ways to Put More Money Towards Your Debt
- Withdraw From Your Retirement Fund
- Cash out a Life Insurance Policy
- Settle With Your Creditors
- Go Through Credit Counseling

GOALS

PERSONAL GOALS

_____
_____
_____
_____
_____
_____
_____
_____

FITNESS GOALS

_____
_____
_____
_____
_____
_____
_____
_____

FINANCIAL GOALS

___

SPIRITUAL GOALS

___

LIFE GOALS

___

_____
_____
_____
_____
_____
_____

LOVE GOALS

_____
_____
_____
_____
_____
_____
_____
_____

EDUCATIONAL GOALS

_____
_____
_____
_____
_____
_____
_____
_____

MENTAL HEALTH GOALS

ENTREPRENEUR GOALS

FITNESS TIPS

- Fitness Tip #1: Form is everything! If your form is off, you are bound for injuries.
- Fitness Tip #2: Portion Control is the key to Weight Loss. Servings shouldn't be more than the palm of your hand.
- Fitness Tip #3: Muscle Burns Fat! Strength Train! You don't have to lift heavy, you just have lift consistently...
- Fitness Tip #4: Fitness has 4 components: Strength, Endurance, Balance, and Flexibility
- Fitness Tip #5: Speed is only accomplished through proper technique. The better the technique the faster you will become.
- Fitness Tip #6: Cardio regulates the density of your body fat, but you need Strength Training to keep the density down.
- Fitness Tip #7: The Body requires 3 nutrients: Carbohydrates, Fats and Proteins... The Body needs Carbs for Energy... Fats for Warmth... Proteins for Recovery and Repair
    - Carbs ~ Complex- Breads, Pastas, Starches
    - Simple ~ Fruits and Veggies

    - Fats ~ Nuts, Dairy
    - Proteins ~ Meats and Beans
- Fitness Tip #8: In order to reach your fitness goals you need to embrace the process...

There is NO PROGRESS without a PROCESS..

Retail Price $15.99

Special Quantity Discounts

5-100 Books	$12.95 each
100-999 Books	$5.95 each
1000+ Books	$6.95 each

To Place An Order Contact:

info@penlegacy.com

ABOUT THE AUTHOR

Since 2008, Charron Monaye has been recognized as a Literary Game Changer who doesn't mind adapting words into legacies. She's been awarded Best Independent Author, authored 10 books, co-authored 4, published over 25 new authors, written/produced 3 theatrical productions, contributed to more than 20 book anthologies worldwide, and hired to pen other theatrical scripts, such as Testify, 'Til Death Do Us Part, and Olivia Lost & Turned Out, just to name a few.

Charron was formerly a staff writer for the Philadelphia Association of Paralegals, CNN iReport, and currently serves as a staff writer for the Department of Veteran Affairs, GovLoop.com, and Editor-In-Chief for www.madisonjaye.com. She is preparing to produce her first film, which started out as a book and later adapted into a theatrical production, "Get Out of Your Own Way".

In 2017, she received a Doctorate of Philosophy (Humane Letters) from CICA International University & Seminary. Just recently, she had the opportunity to hone her writing skills by studying under television producer, screenwriter, and author Shonda Rhimes and NAACP Image Award Author Victoria Christopher Murray.

Charron is an active member of Zeta Phi Beta Sorority, Incorporated and Order of Eastern Star

Books Published By Pen Legacy Publishing

Journals/Guides

Boss Moves Start with You: 2018 Self-Reflection Journal & Vision Planner
by Briana McKnight

Maximizing Your Tax Refund Made Easy!
by Khristina Barnes

Book Anthologies

Bruised, Broken, and Blessed: Life Changing Stories That Will Ignite Hope, Elevate Personal Growth, and Confirm Your Greatness compiled by Charron Monaye & Shontaye Hawkins

Get Out of Your Own Way: Overcoming Adversity to Live In Your Truth Out Loud compiled by Charron Monaye

Inspirational/Non-Fiction

Respect Your Choices: Finding Balance in Success by Vaughn McNeill

Let Me Tell You Like I Told Myself: Love's Truth Never Changes by Summer Willow Fitch

The Power of Shut Up by Lisa Dove Washington

Parenting/Caregiver

From CAREFREE to CAREGIVER: A 31-Day Devotional to Balance, Encourage, and Support You in Your New Role by Teraleen Campbell

Fiction

Leonard Smith by AJ Harrison

Memoirs

The Black Blood in My Heart by La'Mena Marie

The Shadow in My Eyes by Deborah Rose

The Woodshed by Jaguar Wright

How I Survived Without Chemo Therapy: One Woman's Story from Diagnosed to Thriving by Sabrina Moore

Stop Being a Doormat & Start Being a Boss by Toni Moore

Books are available on Amazon, Barnes N Noble, Books A Million, Wal-Mart, Penlegacy.com

www.ingramcontent.com/pod-product-compliance
Lightning Source LLC
Chambersburg PA
CBHW050556300426
44112CB00013B/1944